ASOLANDO

FANCIES AND FACTS

BY

ROBERT BROWNING

Author's Edition

BOSTON AND NEW YORK
HOUGHTON, MIFFLIN AND COMPANY
The Riverside Press, Cambridge
1890

The Riverside Press, Cambridge, Mass., U. S. A.
Electrotyped and Printed by H. O. Houghton & Company.

Robert Browning,

TO MRS. ARTHUR BRONSON.

To whom but you, dear Friend, should I dedicate verses — some few written, all of them supervised, in the comfort of your presence, and with yet another experience of the gracious hospitality now bestowed on me since so many a year, — adding a charm even to my residences at Venice, and leaving me little regret for the surprise and delight at my visits to Asolo in bygone days?

I unite, you will see, the disconnected poems by a title-name popularly ascribed to the inventiveness of the ancient secretary of Queen Cornaro whose palace-tower still overlooks us: *Asolare* — "to disport in the open air, amuse one's self at random." The objection that such a word nowhere occurs in the works of the Cardinal is hardly important — Bembo was too thorough a purist to conserve in print a term which in talk he might possibly toy with: but the word is more likely derived from a Spanish source. I use it for love of the place, and in requital of your pleasant assurance that an early poem of mine first attracted you thither — where and elsewhere, at La Mura as Cà Alvisi, may all happiness attend you!

Gratefully and affectionately yours,

R. B.

Asolo: *October* 15, 1889.

CONTENTS.

―――――

CONTENTS.

ASOLANDO.

PROLOGUE.

" THE Poet's age is sad: for why?
   In youth, the natural world could show
No common object but his eye
   At once involved with alien glow —
His own soul's iris-bow.

" And now a flower is just a flower:
   Man, bird, beast are but beast, bird, man —
Simply themselves, uncinct by dower
   Of dyes which, when life's day began,
Round each in glory ran."

Friend, did you need an optic glass,
   Which were your choice? A lens to drape
In ruby, emerald, chrysopras,

Each object — or reveal its shape
Clear outlined, past escape,

The naked very thing? — so clear
  That, when you had the chance to gaze,
You found its inmost self appear
  Through outer seeming — truth ablaze,
Not falsehood's fancy-haze?

How many a year, my Asolo,
  Since — one step just from sea to land —
I found you, loved yet feared you so —
  For natural objects seemed to stand
Palpably fire-clothed! No —

No mastery of mine o'er these!
  Terror with beauty, like the Bush
Burning but unconsumed. Bend knees,
  Drop eyes to earthward! Language? Tush!
Silence 't is awe decrees.

And now? The lambent flame is — where?
  Lost from the naked world: earth, sky,
Hill, vale, tree, flower, — Italia's rare
  O'er-running beauty crowds the eye —
But flame? The Bush is bare.

Hill, vale, tree, flower — they stand distinct,
    Nature to know and name.   What then?
A Voice spoke thence which straight unlinked
    Fancy from fact: see, all's in ken:
Has once my eyelid winked?

No, for the purged ear apprehends
    Earth's import, not the eye late dazed:
The Voice said, "Call my works thy friends!
    At Nature dost thou shrink amazed?
God is it who transcends."

    ASOLO: *Sept. 6, 1889.*

ROSNY.

Woe, he went galloping into the war,
  Clara, Clara!
Let us two dream: shall he 'scape with a scar?
 Scarcely disfigurement, rather a grace
Making for manhood which nowise we mar:
 See, while I kiss it, the flush on his face —
  Rosny, Rosny!

Light does he laugh: " With your love in my soul " —
  (Clara, Clara!)
" How could I other than — sound, safe, and whole —
 Cleave who opposed me asunder, yet stand
Scatheless beside you, as, touching love's goal,
 Who won the race kneels, craves reward at your
   hand —
  Rosny, Rosny?"

Ay, but if certain who envied should see!
  Clara, Clara,
Certain who simper: " The hero for me

Hardly of life were so chary as miss
Death — death and fame — that 's love's guerdon when
      She
  Boasts, proud bereaved one, her choice fell on this
    Rosny, Rosny ! "

So, — go on dreaming, — he lies mid a heap
      (Clara, Clara,)
Of the slain by his hand : what is death but a sleep ?
  Dead, with my portrait displayed on his breast :
Love wrought his undoing : " No prudence could keep
  The love-maddened wretch from his fate."   That is
      best,
    Rosny, Rosny !

DUBIETY.

I WILL be happy if but for once :
  Only help me, Autumn weather,
Me and my cares to screen, ensconce
  In luxury's sofa-lap of leather!

Sleep ? Nay, comfort — with just a cloud
  Suffusing day too clear and bright :
Eve's essence, the single drop allowed
  To sully, like milk, Noon's water-white.

Let gauziness shade, not shroud, — adjust,
  Dim and not deaden, — somehow sheathe
Aught sharp in the rough world's busy thrust,
  If it reach me through dreaming's vapor-wreath.

Be life so, all things ever the same!
  For, what has disarmed the world ? Outside,
Quiet and peace : inside, nor blame
  Nor want, nor wish whate'er betide.

What is it like that has happened before?
   A dream?   No dream, more real by much.
A vision?   But fanciful days of yore
   Brought many: mere musing seems not such.

Perhaps but a memory, after all!
   — Of what came once when a woman leant
To feel for my brow where her kiss might fall.
   Truth ever, truth only the excellent!

NOW.

OUT of your whole life give but a moment!
All of your life that has gone before,
All to come after it, — so you ignore,
So you make perfect the present, — condense,
In a rapture of rage, for perfection's endowment,
Thought and feeling and soul and sense —
Merged in a moment which gives me at last
You around me for once, you beneath me, above me —
Me — sure that despite of time future, time past, —
This tick of our life-time's one moment you love me!
How long such suspension may linger? Ah, Sweet —
The moment eternal — just that and no more —
When ecstasy's utmost we clutch at the core
While cheeks burn, arms open, eyes shut and lips meet!

HUMILITY.

WHAT girl but, having gathered flowers,
Stript the beds and spoilt the bowers,
From the lapful light she carries
Drops a careless bud ? — nor tarries
To regain the waif and stray :
" Store enough for home " — she 'll say.

So say I too : give your lover
Heaps of loving — under, over,
Whelm him — make the one the wealthy !
Am I all so poor who — stealthy
Work it was ! — picked up what fell :
Not the worst bud — who can tell ?

POETICS.

" So say the foolish ! "   Say the foolish so, Love?
  "Flower she is, my rose " — or else, " My very swan
      is she " —
Or perhaps, " Yon maid-moon, blessing earth below,
      Love,
  Thou art thou! " — to them, belike : no such vain
      words from me.

" Hush, rose, blush! no balm like breath," I chide it :
  " Bend thy neck its best, swan, — hers the whiter
      curve ! "
Be the moon the moon : my Love I place beside it :
  What is she?   Her human self, — no lower word
      will serve.

SUMMUM BONUM.

ALL the breath and the bloom of the year in the bag
    of one bee :
  All the wonder and wealth of the mine in the heart
    of one gem :
In the core of one pearl all the shade and the shine of
    the sea :
  Breath and bloom, shade and shine, — wonder,
    wealth, and — how far above them —
        Truth, that 's brighter than gem,
        Trust, that 's purer than pearl, —
Brightest truth, purest trust in the universe — all were
    for me
        In the kiss of one girl.

A PEARL, A GIRL.

A SIMPLE ring with a single stone
   To the vulgar eye no stone of price:
Whisper the right word, that alone —
   Forth starts a sprite, like fire from ice,
And lo, you are lord (says an Eastern scroll)
Of heaven and earth, lord whole and sole
   Through the power in a pearl.

A woman ('t is I this time that say)
   With little the world counts worthy praise:
Utter the true word — out and away
   Escapes her soul: I am wrapt in blaze,
Creation's lord, of heaven and earth
Lord whole and sole — by a minute's birth —
   Through the love in a girl!

SPECULATIVE.

OTHERS may need new life in Heaven —
　　Man, Nature, Art — made new, assume!
Man with new mind old sense to leaven,
　　Nature — new light to clear old gloom,
Art that breaks bounds, gets soaring-room.

I shall pray: " Fugitive as precious —
　　Minutes which passed, — return, remain!
Let earth's old life once more enmesh us,
　　You with old pleasure, me — old pain,
So we but meet nor part again! "

WHITE WITCHCRAFT.

IF you and I could change to beasts, what beast should
　　either be?
Shall you and I play Jove for once?　Turn fox then,
　　I decree!
Shy wild sweet stealer of the grapes!　Now do your
　　worst on me!

And thus you think to spite your friend — turned
　　loathsome?　What, a toad?
So, all men shrink and shun me!　Dear men, pursue
　　your road!
Leave but my crevice in the stone, a reptile's fit abode!

Now say your worst, Canidia!　"He's loathsome, I
　　allow:
There may or may not lurk a pearl beneath his puck-
　　ered brow:
But see his eyes that follow mine — love lasts there,
　　anyhow."

BAD DREAMS. I.

LAST night I saw you in my sleep :
   And how your charm of face was changed !
I asked, " Some love, some faith you keep ? "
   You, answered, " Faith gone, love estranged."

Whereat I woke — a twofold bliss :
   Waking was one, but next there came
This other : " Though I felt, for this,
   My heart break, I loved on the same."

BAD DREAMS. II.

You in the flesh and here —
  Your very self! Now, wait!
One word! May I hope or fear?
  Must I speak in love or hate?
Stay while I ruminate!

The fact and each circumstance
  Dare you disown? Not you!
That vast dome, that huge dance,
  And the gloom which overgrew
A — possibly festive crew!

For why should men dance at all —
  Why women — a crowd of both —
Unless they are gay? Strange ball —
  Hands and feet plighting troth,
Yet partners enforced and loth!

Of who danced there, no shape
  Did I recognize : thwart, perverse,

Each grasped each, past escape
   In a whirl or weary or worse:
Man's sneer met woman's curse,

While he and she toiled as if
   Their guardian set galley-slaves
To supple chained limbs grown stiff:
   Unmanacled trulls and knaves —
The lash for who misbehaves!

And a gloom was, all the while,
   Deeper and deeper yet
O'ergrowing the rank and file
   Of that army of haters — set
To mimic love's fever-fret.

By the wall-side close I crept,
   Avoiding the livid maze,
And, safely so far, outstepped
   On a chamber — a chapel, says
My memory or betrays —

Closet-like, kept aloof
   From unseemly witnessing
What sport made floor and roof

Of the Devil's palace ring
While his Damned amused their king.

Ay, for a low lamp burned,
   And a silence lay about
What I, in the midst, discerned
   Though dimly till, past doubt,
'T was a sort of throne stood out —

High seat with steps, at least:
   And the topmost step was filled
By — whom?   What vestured priest?
   A stranger to me, — his guild,
His cult, unreconciled

To my knowledge how guild and cult
   Are clothed in this world of ours:
I pondered, but no result
   Came to — unless that Giaours
So worship the Lower Powers.

When suddenly who entered?
   Who knelt — did you guess I saw?
Who — raising that face where centred
   Allegiance to love and law
So lately — off-casting awe,

Down-treading reserve, away
  Thrusting respect . . . but mine
Stands firm — firm still shall stay!
  Ask Satan! for I decline
To tell — what I saw, in fine!

Yet here in the flesh you come —
  Your same self, form and face, —
In the eyes, mirth still at home!
  On the lips, that commonplace
Perfection of honest grace!

Yet your errand is — needs must be —
  To palliate — well, explain,
Expurgate in some degree
  Your soul of its ugly stain.
Oh, you — the good in grain —

How was it your white took tinge?
  " A mere dream " — never object!
Sleep leaves a door on hinge
  Whence soul, ere our flesh suspect,
Is off and away : detect

Her vagaries when loose, who can!
  Be she pranksome, be she prude,

Disguise with the day began :
  With the night — ah, what ensued
From draughts of a drink hell-brewed ?

Then She : " What a queer wild dream !
  And perhaps the best fun is —
Myself had its fellow — I seem
  Scarce awake from yet.   'T was this —
Shall I tell you ?   First, a kiss !

" For the fault was just your own, —
  'T is myself expect apology :
You warned me to let alone
  (Since our studies were mere philology)
That ticklish (you said) Anthology.

" So, I dreamed that I passed *exam*
  Till a question posed me sore :
Who translated this epigram
  By — an author we best ignore ? '
And I answered, ' Hannah More ' ! "

BAD DREAMS. III.

THIS was my dream : I saw a Forest
   Old as the earth, no track nor trace
Of unmade man.   Thou, Soul, explorest —
   Though in a trembling rapture — space
Immeasurable ! Shrubs, turned trees,
Trees that touch heaven, support its frieze
Studded with sun and moon and star :
While — oh, the enormous growths that bar
Mine eye from penetrating past
   Their tangled twine where lurks — nay, lives
Royally lone, some brute-type cast
   I' the rough, time cancels, man forgives.

On, Soul !   I saw a lucid City
   Of architectural device
Every way perfect.   Pause for pity,
   Lightning ! nor leave a cicatrice
On those bright marbles, dome and spire,
Structures palatial, — streets which mire
Dares not defile, paved all too fine

For human footsteps' smirch, not thine —
Proud solitary traverser,
   My Soul, of silent lengths of way —
With what ecstatic dread, aver,
   Lest life start sanctioned by thy stay!

Ah, but the last sight was the hideous!
   A City, yes, — a Forest, true, —
But each devouring each. Perfidious
   Snake-plants had strangled what I knew
Was a pavilion once: each oak
Held on his horns some spoil he broke
By surreptitiously beneath
Upthrusting: pavements, as with teeth,
Griped huge weed widening crack and split
   In squares and circles stone-work erst.
Oh, Nature — good! Oh, Art — no whit
   Less worthy! Both in one — accurst!

BAD DREAMS. IV.

IT happened thus : my slab, though new,
　　Was getting weather-stained, — beside,
Herbage, balm, peppermint o'ergrew
　　Letter and letter : till you tried
Somewhat, the Name was scarce descried.

That strong stern man my lover came :
　　— Was he my lover ?　Call him, pray,
My life's cold critic bent on blame
　　Of all poor I could do or say
To make me worth his love one day —

One far day when, by diligent
　　And dutiful amending faults,
Foibles, all weaknesses which went
　　To challenge and excuse assaults
Of culture wronged by taste that halts —

Discrepancies should mar no plan
　　Symmetric of the qualities

Claiming respect from — say — a man
   That's strong and stern.   " Once more he pries
Into me with those critic eyes ! "

No question ! so — " Conclude, condemn
   Each failure my poor self avows !
Leave to its fate all you contemn !
   There 's Solomon's selected spouse :
Earth needs must hold such maids — choose them ! "

Why, he was weeping !   Surely gone
   Sternness and strength : with eyes to ground
And voice a broken monotone —
   " Only be as you were !   Abound
In foibles, faults, — laugh, robed and crowned

" As Folly's veriest queen, — care I
   One feather-fluff ?   Look pity, Love,
On prostrate me — your foot shall try
   This forehead's use — mount thence above,
And reach what Heaven you dignify ! "

Now, what could bring such change about ?
   The thought perplexed : till, following
His gaze upon the ground, — why, out

Came all the secret !   So, a thing
  Thus simple has deposed my king !

For, spite of weeds that strove to spoil
  Plain reading on the lettered slab,
My name was clear enough — no soil
  Effaced the date when one chance stab
Of scorn . . . if only ghosts might blab !

INAPPREHENSIVENESS.

WE two stood simply friend-like side by side,
Viewing a twilight country far and wide,
Till she at length broke silence. " How it towers
Yonder, the ruin o'er this vale of ours !
The West's faint flare behind it so relieves
Its rugged outline — sight perhaps deceives,
Or I could almost fancy that I see
A branch wave plain — belike some wind-sown tree
Chance-rooted where a missing turret was.
What would I give for the perspective glass
At home, to make out if 't is really so !
Has Ruskin noticed here at Asolo
That certain weed-growths on the ravaged wall
Seem " . . . something that I could not say at all,
My thought being rather — as absorbed she sent
Look onward after look from eyes distent
With longing to reach Heaven's gate left ajar —
" Oh, fancies that might be, oh, facts that are !
What of a wilding ?   By you stands, and may
So stand unnoticed till the Judgment Day,

One who, if once aware that your regard
Claimed what his heart holds, — woke, as from its
   sward
The flower, the dormant passion, so to speak —
Then what a rush of life would startling wreak
Revenge on your inapprehensive stare
While, from the ruin and the West's faint flare,
You let your eyes meet mine, touch what you term
Quietude — that's an universe in germ —
The dormant passion needing but a look
To burst into immense life ! "

        " No, the book
Which noticed how the wall-growths wave," said she,
" Was not by Ruskin."

       I said, " Vernon Lee ? "

WHICH?

So, the three Court-ladies began
    Their trial of who judged best
    In esteeming the love of a man:
Who preferred with most reason was thereby con-
    fessed
Boy-Cupid's exemplary catcher and cager;
An Abbé crossed legs to decide on the wager.

    First the Duchesse: " Mine for me —
        Who were it but God's for Him,
        And the King's for — who but he?
    Both faithful and loyal, one grace more shall brim
His cup with perfection : a lady's true lover,
He holds — save his God and his king — none above
    her."

    " I require " — outspoke the Marquise —
        " Pure thoughts, ay, but also fine deeds :
        Play the paladin must he, to please
My whim, and — to prove my knight's service ex-
    ceeds

Your saint's and your loyalist's praying and kneel-
    ing —
Show wounds, each wide mouth to my mercy appeal-
    ing."

    Then the Comtesse : " My choice be a wretch,
      Mere losel in body and soul,
    Thrice accurst ! What care I, so he stretch
Arms to me his sole saviour, love's ultimate goal,
Out of earth and men's noise — names of ' infidel,'
      ' traitor,'
Cast up at him? Crown me, crown's adjudicator ! "

    And the Abbé uncrossed his legs,
      Took snuff, a reflective pinch,
    Broke silence: " The question begs
Much pondering ere I pronounce. Shall I flinch?
The love which to one and one only has reference
Seems terribly like what perhaps gains God's prefer-
      ence."

THE CARDINAL AND THE DOG.

CRESCENZIO, the Pope's Legate at the High Council,
    Trent,
— Year Fifteen hundred twenty-two, March Twenty-
    five — intent
On writing letters to the Pope till late into the night,
Rose, weary, to refresh himself, and saw a monstrous
    sight:
(I give mine Author's very words: he penned, I re-
    indite.)

A black Dog of vast bigness, eyes flaming, ears that
    hung
Down to the very ground almost, into the chamber
    sprung
And made directly for him, and laid himself right
    under
The table where Crescenzio wrote — who called in
    fear and wonder
His servants in the ante-room, commanded every one
To look for and find out the beast: but, looking, they
    found none.

The Cardinal fell melancholy, then sick, soon after
    died : ·
And at Verona, as he lay on his death-bed, he cried
Aloud to drive away the Dog that leapt on his bed-
    side.
Heaven keep us Protestants from harm : the rest . . .
    no ill betide !

THE POPE AND THE NET.

WHAT, he on whom our voices unanimously ran,
Made Pope at our last Conclave? Full low his life
    began:
His father earned the daily bread as just a fisher-
    man.

So much the more his boy minds book, gives proof of
    mother-wit,
Becomes first Deacon, and then Priest, then Bishop:
    see him sit
No less than Cardinal erelong, while no one cries
    " Unfit! "

But some one smirks, some other smiles, jogs elbow
    and nods head:
Each winks at each: " 'I-faith, a rise! Saint Peter's
    net, instead
Of sword and keys, is come in vogue! " You think
    he blushes red?

Not he, of humble holy heart! "Unworthy me!" he
    sighs:
"From fisher's drudge to Church's prince — it is in-
    deed a rise :
So, here 's my way to keep the fact forever in my
    eyes !"

And straightway in his palace-hall, where commonly
    is set
Some coat-of-arms, some portraiture ancestral, lo, we
    met
His mean estate's reminder in his fisher-father's net !

Which step conciliates all and some, stops cavil in a
    trice :
" The humble holy heart that holds of new-born pride
    no spice !
He 's just the saint to choose for Pope!" Each adds,
    " 'T is my advice."

So, Pope he was : and when we flocked — its sacred
    slipper on —
To kiss his foot, we lifted eyes, alack the thing was
    gone —
That guarantee of lowlihead, — eclipsed that star
    which shone !

Each eyed his fellow, one and all kept silence.   I
   cried, " Pish !
I 'll make me spokesman for the rest, express the com-
   mon wish.
Why, Father. is the net removed ? " " Son, it hath
   caught the fish."

THE BEAN–FEAST.

HE was the man — Pope Sixtus, that Fifth, that
    swineherd's son :
He knew the right thing, did it, and thanked God
    when 't was done :
But of all he had to thank for, my fancy somehow
    leans
To thinking, what most moved him was a certain meal
    on beans.

For one day, as his wont was, in just enough dis-
    guise
As he went exploring wickedness, — to see with his
    own eyes
If law had due observance in the city's entrail dark
As well as where, i' the open, crime stood an obvious
    mark, —

He chanced, in a blind alley, on a tumble-down once
    house
Now hovel, vilest structure in Rome the ruinous :

And, as his tact impelled him, Sixtus adventured
    bold,
To learn how lowliest subjects bore hunger, toil, and
    cold.

There sat they at high-supper — man and wife, lad
    and lass,
Poor as you please, but cleanly all and care-free: pain
    that was
— Forgotten, pain as sure to be let bide aloof its
    time, —
Mightily munched the brave ones — what mattered
    gloom or grime?

Said Sixtus, " Feast, my children ! who works hard
    needs eat well.
I'm just a supervisor, would hear what you can
    tell.
Do any wrongs want righting? The Father tries his
    best,
But, since he's only mortal, sends such as I to test
The truth of all that's told him — how folk like you
    may fare:
Come ! — only don't stop eating — when mouth has
    words to spare —

"You " — smiled he — " play the spokesman, bell-
    wether of the flock!
Are times good, masters gentle? Your grievances un-
    lock !
How of your work and wages? — pleasures, if such
    may be —
Pains, as such are for certain." Thus smiling ques-
    tioned he.

But somehow, spite of smiling, awe stole upon the
    group —
An inexpressible surmise: why should a priest thus
    stoop —
Pry into what concerned folk? Each visage fell.
    Aware,
Cries Sixtus interposing : " Nay, children, have no
    care!

" Fear nothing! Who employs me requires the
    plain truth. Pelf
Beguiles who should inform me : so, I inform myself.
See!" And he threw his hood back, let the close
    vesture ope,
Showed face, and where on tippet the cross lay:
    't was the Pope.

Imagine the joyful wonder! " How shall the like
 of us —
Poor souls — requite such blessing of our rude bean-
 feast ? "   " Thus —
Thus amply ! " laughed Pope Sixtus.   " I early rise,
 sleep late :
Who works may eat : they tempt me, your beans
 there : spare a plate ! "

Down sat he on the door-step : 't was they this time
 said grace :
He ate up the last mouthful, wiped lips, and then,
 with face
Turned heavenward, broke forth thankful : " Not
 now, that earth obeys
Thy word in mine, that through me the peoples
 know Thy ways —

But that Thy care extendeth to Nature's homely
 wants,
And, while man's mind is strengthened, Thy good-
 ness nowise scants
Man's body of its comfort, — that I whom kings
 and queens
Crouch to, pick crumbs from off my table, relish
 beans !

The thunders I but seem to launch, there plain Thy
    hand all see:
That I have appetite, digest, and thrive — that boon's
    for me."

MUCKLE-MOUTH MEG.

FROWNED the Laird on the Lord: "So, red-handed
    I catch thee?
Death-doomed by our Law of the Border!
We've a gallows outside and a chiel to dispatch thee:
    Who trespasses — hangs: all's in order."

He met frown with smile, did the young English
    gallant:
Then the Laird's dame: "Nay, Husband, I beg!
He's comely: be merciful! Grace for the callant
    — If he marries our Muckle-mouth Meg!

"No mile-wide-mouthed monster of yours do I marry:
    Grant rather the gallows!" laughed he.
"Foul fare kith and kin of you — why do you tarry?"
    "To tame your fierce temper!" quoth she.

"Shove him quick in the Hole, shut him fast for a
    week:
Cold, darkness, and hunger work wonders:

Who lion-like roars now, mouse-fashion will squeak,
  And ' it rains '·soon succeed to ' it thunders.' "

A week did he bide in the cold and the dark
  — Not hunger: for duly at morning
In flitted a lass, and a voice like a lark
  Chirped, "Muckle-mouth Meg still ye're scorn-
     ing?

" Go hang, but here's parritch to hearten ye first!"
  " Did Meg's muckle-mouth boast within some
Such music as yours, mine should match it or burst:
  No frog-jaws! So tell folk, my Winsome!"

Soon week came to end, and, from Hole's door set
     wide,
  Out he marched, and there waited the lassie:
" Yon gallows, or Muckle-mouth Meg for a bride!
  Consider! Sky's blue and turf's grassy:

" Life's sweet: shall I say ye wed Muckle-mouth
     Meg?"
  " Not I," quoth the stout heart: "too eerie
The mouth that can swallow a bubblyjock's egg:
  Shall I let it munch mine? Never, Dearie!

" Not   Muckle - mouth   Meg ?   Wow,   the   obstinate
    man !
  Perhaps he would rather wed me ! "
" Ay, would he — with just for a dowry your can ! "
  " I 'm Muckle-mouth Meg," chirruped she.

" Then so — so — so — so — " as he kissed her apace —
  " Will I widen thee out till thou turnest
From Margaret Minnikin-mou', by God's grace,
  To Muckle-mouth Meg in good earnest ! "

ARCADES AMBO.

A. You blame me that I ran away?
      Why, Sir, the enemy advanced :
  Balls flew about, and — who can say
      But one, if I stood firm, had glanced
  In my direction ?   Cowardice ?
  I only know we don't live twice,
  Therefore — shun death, is my advice.

B. Shun death at all risks ?   Well, at some !
      True, I myself, Sir, though I scold
  The cowardly, by no means come
      Under reproof as overbold
  — I, who would have no end of brutes
  Cut up alive to guess what suits
  My case and saves my toe from shoots.

THE LADY AND THE PAINTER.

She. Yet womanhood you reverence,
            So you profess !
He.   With heart and soul.
She. Of which fact this is evidence !
            To help Art-study, — for some dole
            Of certain wretched shillings, — you
            Induce a woman — virgin too —
            To strip and stand stark-naked ?
He.   True.

She. Nor feel you so degrade her ?
He.   What
            — (Excuse the interruption) — clings
            Half-savage-like around your hat ?
She.   Ah, do they please you ?   Wild-bird-wings !
            Next season, — Paris-prints assert, —
            We must go feathered to the skirt :
            My modiste keeps on the alert.

            Owls, hawks, jays — swallows most approve . . .
He.   Dare I speak plainly ?

She. Oh, I trust!

He. Then, Lady Blanche, it less would move
  In heart and soul of me disgust
  Did you strip off those spoils you wear,
  And stand — for thanks, not shillings — bare,
  To help Art like my Model there.
  She well knew what absolved her — praise
  In me for God's surpassing good,
  Who granted to my reverent gaze
  A type of purest womanhood.
  You — clothed with murder of His best
  Of harmless beings — stand the test!
  What is it *you* know?

She. That you jest!

PONTE DELL' ANGELO, VENICE.

STOP rowing !   This one of our bye-canals
O'er a certain bridge you have to cross
That 's named, " Of the Angel " : listen why !
The name " Of the Devil " too much appals
Venetian acquaintance, so — his the loss,
While the gain goes . . . look on high !

An angel visibly guards yon house :
Above each scutcheon — a pair — stands he,
Enfolds them with droop of either wing :
The family's fortune were perilous
Did he thence depart — you will soon agree,
If I hitch into verse the thing.

For, once on a time, this house belonged
To a lawyer of note, with law and to spare,
But also with overmuch lust of gain :
In the matter of law you were nowise wronged,
But alas for the lucre !   He picked you bare
To the bone.   Did folk complain ?

" I exact," growled he, " work's rightful due :
'T is folk seek me, not I seek them.
Advice at its price ! They succeed or fail,
Get law in each case — and a lesson too :
Keep clear of the Courts — is advice *ad rem :*
They 'll remember, I 'll be bail ! "

So, he pocketed fee without a qualm.
What reason for squeamishness ? Labor done,
To play he betook him with lightened heart,
Ate, drank, and made merry with song or psalm,
Since the yoke of the Church is an easy one —
Fits neck nor causes smart.

Brief : never was such an extortionate
Rascal — the word has escaped my teeth !
And yet — (all 's down in a book no ass
Indited, believe me !) — this reprobate
Was punctual at prayer - time : gold lurked be-
        neath
Alloy of the rankest brass.

For, play the extortioner as he might,
Fleece folk each day and all day long,
There was this redeeming circumstance :

He never lay down to sleep at night
But he put up a prayer first, brief yet strong,
" Our Lady avert mischance ! "

Now it happened at close of a fructuous week,
" I must ask," quoth he, " some Saint to dine :
I want that widow well out of my ears
With her ailing and wailing.   Who bade her seek
Redress at my hands ? ' She was wronged ! ' Folk
      whine
If to Law wrong right appears.

" Matteo da Bascio — he 's my man !
No less than Chief of the Capucins :
His presence will surely suffumigate
My house — fools think lies under a ban
If somebody loses what somebody wins.
Hark, there he knocks at the grate !

" Come in, thou blessed of Mother Church !
I go and prepare — to bid, that is,
My trusty and diligent servitor
Get all things in readiness.   Vain the search
Through Venice for one to compare with this
My model of ministrants : for —

" For — once again, nay, three times over,
My helpmate 's an ape ! so intelligent,
I train him to drudge at household work :
He toils and he moils, I live in clover :
Oh, you shall see !   There 's a goodly scent —
From his cooking, or I 'm a Turk !

" Scarce need to descend and supervise :
I 'll do it, however : wait here awhile ! "
So, down to the kitchen gayly scuttles
Our host, nor notes the alarmed surmise
Of the holy man.   " O depth of guile !
He blindly guzzles and guttles,

" While — who is it dresses the food and pours
The liquor ?   Some fiend — I make no doubt —
In likeness of — which of the loathly brutes ?
An ape !   Where hides he ?   No bull that gores,
No bear that hugs — 't is the mock and flout
Of an ape, fiend's face that suits.

" So — out with thee, creature, wherever thou hidest !
I charge thee, by virtue of . . . right do I judge !
There skulks he perdue, crouching under the bed.
Well done !   What, forsooth, in beast's shape thou
        confidest ?

I know and would name thee but that I begrudge
Breath spent on such carrion.   Instead —

" I adjure thee by ——"   " Stay ! " laughed the por-
          tent that rose
From floor up to ceiling : " No need to adjure !
See Satan in person, late ape by command
Of Him thou adjurest in vain.   A saint's nose
Scents brimstone though incense be burned for a lure.
Yet, hence ! for I 'm safe, understand !

" 'T is my charge to convey to fit punishment's place
This lawyer, my liegeman, for cruelty wrought
On his clients, the widow and orphan, poor souls
He has plagued by exactions which proved law's dis-
          grace,
Made equity void and to nothingness brought
God's pity.   Fiends, on with fresh coals ! "

" Stay ! " nowise confounded, withstands Hell its
          match :
" How comes it, were truth in this story of thine,
God's punishment suffered a minute's delay ?
Weeks, months have elapsed since thou squattedst at
          watch

For a spring on thy victim : what caused thee decline
Advantage till challenged to-day ? "

" That challenge I meet with contempt," quoth the
    fiend.
" Thus much I acknowledge : the man's armed in
    mail :
I wait till a joint's loose, then quick ply my claws.
Thy friend's one good custom — he knows not —
    has screened
His flesh hitherto from what else would assail :
At 'Save me, Madonna ! ' I pause.

" That prayer did the losel but once pretermit,
My pounce were upon him. I keep me attent :
He's in safety but till he's caught napping.
    Enough ! "
" Ay, enough ! " smiles the Saint — " for the biter is
    bit,
The spy caught in somnolence. Vanish ! I'm sent
To smooth up what fiends do in rough."

" I vanish ? Through wall or through roof ? " the
    ripost
Grinned gayly. " My orders were — ' Leave not un-
    harmed

The abode of this lawyer!   Do damage to prove
'T was for something thou quittedst the land of the
        lost —
To add to their number this unit!'   Though charmed
From descent there, on earth that's above

"I may haply amerce him."   "So do, and begone,
I command thee!   For, look!   Though there's door-
        way behind
And window before thee, go straight through the
        wall,
Leave a breach in the brickwork, a gap in the stone
For who passes to stare at!"   "Spare speech!   I'm
        resigned:
Here goes!" roared the goblin, as all —

Wide bat-wings, spread arms and legs, tail out
        a-stream,
Crash obstacles went, right and left, as he soared
Or else sank, was clean gone through the hole any-
        how.
The Saint returned thanks: then a satisfied gleam
On the bald polished pate showed that triumph was
        scored.
"To dinner with appetite now!"

Down he trips. "In good time!" smirks the host.
  "Didst thou scent
Rich savor of roast meat? Where hides he, my ape?
Look alive, be alert! He's away to wash plates.
Sit down, Saint! What's here? Dost examine a
  rent
In the napkin thou twistest and twirlest? Agape . . .
Ha, blood is it drips nor abates

"From thy wringing a cloth, late was lavendered fair?
What means such a marvel?" "Just this does it
  mean:
I convince and convict thee of sin!" answers straight
The Saint, wringing on, wringing ever — O rare! —
Blood — blood from a napery snow not more clean.
"A miracle shows thee thy state!

"See — blood thy extortions have wrung from the
  flesh
Of thy clients who, sheep-like, arrived to be shorn,
And left thee — or fleeced to the quick or so flayed
That, behold, their blood gurgles and grumbles afresh
To accuse thee! Ay, down on thy knees, get up
  sworn
To restore! Restitution once made,

" Sin no more!   Dost thou promise?   Absolved, then,
          arise!
Upstairs follow me!   Art amazed at yon breach?
Who battered and shattered and scattered, escape
From thy purlieus obtaining?   That Father of
          Lies
Thou wast wont to extol for his feats, all and each
The Devil's disguised as thine ape!"

Be sure that our lawyer was torn by remorse,
Shed tears in a flood, vowed and swore so to alter
His ways that how else could our Saint but declare
He was cleansed of past sin?   "For sin future — fare
          worse
Thou undoubtedly wilt," warned the Saint, "shouldst
          thou falter
One whit!"   "Oh, for that have no care!

" I am firm in my purposed amendment.   But,
          prithee,
Must ever affront and affright me yon gap?
Who made it for exit may find it of use
For entrance as easy.   If, down in his smithy
He forges me fetters — when heated, mayhap,
He'll up with an armful!   Broke loose —

"How bar him out henceforth?"   "Judiciously
    urged!"
Was the good man's reply.   "How to baulk him is
    plain.
There's nothing the Devil objects to so much,
So speedily flies from, as one of those purged
Of his presence, the angels who erst formed his
    train —
His, their emperor.   Choose one of such!

" Get fashioned his likeness and set him on high
At back of the breach thus adroitly filled up :
Display him as guard of two scutcheons, thy arms :
I warrant no devil attempts to get by
And disturb thee so guarded. Eat, drink, dine, and
    sup,
In thy rectitude, safe from alarms!"

So said and so done.   See, the angel has place
Where the Devil had passage!   All's down in a
    book.
Gainsay me? Consult it! Still faithless? Trust *me?*
Trust Father Boverio who gave me the case
In his Annals — gets of it, by hook or by crook,
Two confirmative witnesses : three

Are surely enough to establish an act:
And thereby we learn — would we ascertain truth —
To trust wise tradition which took, at the time,
Note that served till slow history ventured on fact,
Though folk have their fling at tradition forsooth!
Row, boys, fore and aft, rhyme and chime!

BEATRICE SIGNORINI.

THIS strange thing happened to a painter once:
Viterbo boasts the man among her sons
Of note, I seem to think : his ready tool
Picked up its precepts in Cortona's school —
That 's Pietro Berretini, whom they call
Cortona, these Italians : greatish-small,
Our painter was his pupil, by repute
His match if not his master absolute,
Though whether he spoiled fresco more or less,
And what 's its fortune, scarce repays your guess.
Still, for one circumstance, I save his name
— Francesco Romanelli : do the same !
He went to Rome and painted : there he knew
A wonder of a woman painting too —
For she, at least, was no Cortona's drudge :
Witness that ardent fancy-shape — I judge
A semblance of her soul — she called, " Desire "
With starry front for guide, where sits the fire
She left to brighten Buonarroti's house.
If you see Florence, pay that piece your vows,

Though blockhead Baldinucci's mind, imbued
With monkish morals, bade folk " Drape the nude
And stop the scandal ! " quoth the record prim
I borrow this of : hang his book and him !
At Rome, then, where these fated ones met first,
The blossom of his life had hardly burst
While hers was blooming at full beauty's stand :
No less Francesco — when half-ripe he scanned
Consummate Artemisia — grew one want
To have her his and make her ministrant
With every gift of body and of soul
To him.   In vain.   Her sphery self was whole —
Might only touch his orb at Art's sole point.
Suppose he could persuade her to enjoint
Her life — past, present, future — all in his
At Art's sole point by some explosive kiss
Of love through lips, would love's success defeat
Artistry's haunting curse — the Incomplete ?
Artists no doubt they both were, — what beside
Was she ? who, long had felt heart, soul spread wide
Her life out, knowing much and loving well,
On either side Art's narrow space where fell
Reflection from his own speck : but the germ
Of individual genius — what we term
The very self, the God-gift whence had grown

Heart's life and soul's life, — how make that his own?
Vainly his Art, reflected, smiled in small
On Art's one facet of her ampler ball ;
The rest, touch-free, took in, gave back heaven, earth,
All where he was not.   Hope, well-nigh ere birth
Came to Desire, died off all-unfulfilled.
" What though in Art I stand the abler-skilled,"
(So he conceited : mediocrity
Turns on itself the self-transforming eye)
" If only Art were suing, mine would plead
To purpose : man — by nature I exceed
Woman the bounded : but how much beside
She boasts, would sue in turn and be denied !
Love her ?   My own wife loves me in a sort
That suits us both : she takes the world's report
Of what my work is worth, and, for the rest,
Concedes that, while his consort keeps her nest,
The eagle soars a licensed vagrant, lives
A wide free life which she at least forgives —
Good Beatricé Signorini !   Well
And wisely did I choose her.   But the spell
To subjugate this Artemisia — where ?
She passionless ? — she resolute to care
Nowise beyond the plain sufficiency
Of fact that she is she and I am I

— Acknowledged arbitrator for us both
In her life as in mine which she were loth
Even to learn the laws of?   No, and no,
Twenty times over!   Ay, it must be so:
I for myself, alas!"

                Whereon, instead
Of the checked lover's-utterance — why, he said
— Leaning above her easel: "Flesh is red"
(Or some such just remark) — "by no means white
As Guido's practice teaches: you are right."
Then came the better impulse: "What if pride
Were wisely trampled on, whate'er betide?
If I grow hers, not mine — join lives, confuse
Bodies and spirits, gain her not but lose
Myself to Artemisia?   That were love!
Of two souls — one must bend, one rule above:
If I crouch under proudly, lord turned slave,
Were it not worthier both than if she gave
Herself — in treason to herself — to me?"

And, all the while, he felt it could not be.
Such love were true love: love that way who can!
Some one that's born half woman not whole man:
For man, prescribed man better or man worse,
Why, whether microcosm or universe,

What law prevails alike through great and small,
The world and man — world's miniature we call?
Male is the master. "That way" — smiled and
    sighed
Our true male estimator — "puts her pride
My wife in making me the outlet whence
She learns all Heaven allows : 't is my pretence
To paint : her lord should do what else but paint?
Do I break brushes, cloister me turned saint?
Then, best of all suits sanctity her spouse
Who acts for Heaven, allows and disallows
At pleasure, past appeal, the right, the wrong
In all things. That's my wife's way. But this
    strong
Confident Artemisia — an adept
In Art does she conceit herself? 'Except
In just this instance,' tell her, 'no one draws
More rigidly observant of the laws
Of right design : yet here, — permit me hint, —
If the acromion had a deeper dint,
That shoulder were perfection.' What surprise
— Nay scorn, shoots black fire from those startled
    eyes!
She to be lessoned in design forsooth!
I 'm doomed and done for, since I spoke the truth.

Make my own work the subject of dispute —
Fails it of just perfection absolute
Somewhere?   Those motors, flexors, — don't I know
Ser Santi, styled ' Tirititototo
The pencil-prig,' might blame them?   Yet my wife —
Were he and his nicknamer brought to life,
Tito and Titian, to pronounce again —
Ask her who knows more — I or the great Twain,
Our colorist and draughtsman !

                             " I help her,
Not she helps me ; and neither shall demur
Because my portion is " — he chose to think —
" Quite other than a woman's : I may drink
At many waters, must repose by none —
Rather arise and fare forth, having done
Duty to one new excellence the more,
Abler thereby, though impotent before
So much was gained of knowledge.   Best depart
From this last lady I have learned by heart ! "

Thus he concluded of himself — resigned
To play the man and master : " Man boasts mind :
Woman, man's sport calls mistress, to the same
Does body's suit and service.   Would she claim
— My placid Beatricé-wife — pretence

Even to blame her lord if, going hence,
He wistfully regards one whom — did fate
Concede — he might accept queen, abdicate
Kingship because of ? — one of no meek sort
But masterful as he : man's match in short ?
Oh, there 's no secret I were best conceal !
Bicé shall know ; and should a stray tear steal
From out the blue eye, stain the rose cheek — bah !
A smile, a word's gay reassurance — ah,
With kissing interspersed, — shall make amends,
Turn pain to pleasure."

                        " What, in truth so ends
Abruptly, do you say, our intercourse ? "
Next day, asked Artemisia : " I 'll divorce
Husband and wife no longer.   Go your ways,
Leave Rome !   Viterbo owns no equal, says
The bye-word, for fair women : you, no doubt,
May boast a paragon all specks without,
Using the painter's privilege to choose
Among what 's rarest.   Will your wife refuse
Acceptance from — no rival — of a gift ?
You paint the human figure I make shift
Humbly to reproduce : but, in my hours
Of idlesse, what I fain would paint is — flowers.
Look now ! "

She twitched aside a veiling cloth.
" Here is my keepsake — frame and picture both:
For see, the frame is all of flowers festooned
About an empty space, — left thus, to wound
No natural susceptibility :
How can I guess?   'T is you must fill, not I,
The central space with — her whom you like best !
That is your business, mine has been the rest.
But judge ! ' "

How judge them?   Each of us, in flowers,
Chooses his love, allies it with past hours,
Old meetings, vanished forms and faces: no —
Here let each favorite unmolested blow
For one heart's homage, no tongue's banal praise,
Whether the rose appealingly bade " Gaze
Your fill on me, sultana who dethrone
The gaudy tulip ! " or 't was " Me alone
Rather do homage to, who lily am,
No unabashed rose ! " " Do I vainly cram
My cup with sweets, your jonquil? "   " Why forget
Vernal endearments with the violet ? "
So they contested yet concerted, all
As one, to circle round about, enthral
Yet, self-forgetting, push to prominence
The midmost wonder, gained no matter whence.

There's a tale extant, in a book I conned
Long years ago, which treats of things beyond
The common, antique times and countries queer
And customs strange to match. " 'T is said, last year,"
(Recounts my author) " that the King had mind
To view his kingdom — guessed at from behind
A palace-window hitherto.   Announced
No sooner was such purpose than 't was pounced
Upon by all the ladies of the land —
Loyal but light of life : they formed a band
Of loveliest ones but lithest also, since
Proudly they all combined to bear their prince.
Backs joined to breasts, — arms, legs, — nay, ankles,
        wrists,
Hands, feet, I know not by what turns and twists,
So interwoven lay that you believed
'T was one sole beast of burden which received
The monarch on its back, of breadth not scant,
Since fifty girls made one white elephant.
So with the fifty flowers which shapes and hues
Blent, as I tell, and made one fast yet loose
Mixture of beauties, composite, distinct
No less in each combining flower that linked
With flower to form a fit environment
For — whom might be the painter's heart's intent
Thus, in the midst enhaloed, to enshrine ?

"This glory-guarded middle space — is mine?
For me to fill?"

              "For you, my Friend! We part,
Never perchance to meet again. Your Art —
What if I mean it — so to speak — shall wed
My own, be witness of the life we led
When sometimes it has seemed our souls near
      found
Each one the other as its mate — unbound
Had yours been haply from the better choice
— Beautiful Bicé: 't is the common voice,
The crowning verdict. Make whom you like best
Queen of the central space, and manifest
Your predilection for what flower beyond
All flowers finds favor with you. I am fond
Of — say — yon rose's rich predominance,
While you — what wonder? — more affect the glance
The gentler violet from its leafy screen
Ventures: so — choose your flower and paint your
      queen!"

Oh but the man was ready, head as hand,
Instructed and adroit. "Just as you stand,
Stay and be made — would Nature but relent —
By Art immortal!"

                   Every implement
In tempting reach — a palette primed, each squeeze
Of oil-paint in its proper patch — with these,
Brushes, a veritable sheaf to grasp !
He worked as he had never dared.

                               " Unclasp
My Art from yours who can ! " — he cried at length,
As down he threw the pencil — " Grace from Strength
Dissociate, from your flowery fringe detach
My face of whom it frames, — the feat will match
With that of Time should Time from me extract
Your memory, Artemisia ! " And in fact, —
What with the pricking impulse, sudden glow
Of soul — head, hand coöperated so
That face was worthy of its frame, 't is said —
Perfect, suppose !

                      They parted.   Soon instead
Of Rome was home, — of Artemisia — well,
The placid-perfect wife.   And it befell
That after the first incontestably
Blessedest of all blisses (— wherefore try
Your patience with embracings and the rest
Due from Calypso's all-unwilling guest
To his Penelope ?) — there somehow came
The coolness which as duly follows flame.

So, one day, " What if we inspect the gifts
My Art has gained us ? "

                              Now the wife uplifts
A casket-lid, now tries a medal's chain
Round her own lithe neck, fits a ring in vain
— Too loose on the fine finger, — vows and swears
The jewel with two pendent pearls like pears
Betters a lady's bosom — witness else!
And so forth, while Ulysses smiles.

                                    " Such spells
Subdue such natures — sex must worship toys
— Trinkets and trash : yet, ah, quite other joys
Must stir from sleep the passionate abyss
Of — such an one as her I know — not this
My gentle consort with the milk for blood!
Why, did it chance that in a careless mood
(In those old days, gone — never to return —
When we talked — she to teach and I to learn)
I dropped a word, a hint which might imply
Consorts exist — how quick flashed fire from eye,
Brow blackened, lip was pinched by furious lip!
I needed no reminder of my slip :
One warning taught me wisdom.   Whereas here . . .
Aha, a sportive fancy !   Eh, what fear
Of harm to follow ?   Just a whim indulged!

" My Beatricé, there 's an undivulged
Surprise in store for you: the moment 's fit
For letting loose a secret: out with it!
Tributes to worth, you rightly estimate
These gifts of Prince and Bishop, Church and State:
Yet, may I tell you? Tastes so disagree!
There 's one gift, preciousest of all to me,
I doubt if you would value as well worth
The obvious sparkling gauds that men unearth
For toy-cult mainly of you womankind ;
Such make you marvel, I concede : while blind
The sex proves to the greater marvel here
I veil to baulk its envy. Be sincere!
Say, should you search creation far and wide,
Was ever face like this ? "

                    He drew aside
The veil, displayed the flower-framed portrait kept
For private delectation.
                   No adept
In florist's lore more accurately named
And praised or, as appropriately, blamed
Specimen after specimen of skill,
Than Bicé. " Rightly placed the daffodil —
Scarcely so right the blue germander. Gray

Good mouse-ear! Hardly your auricula
Is powdered white enough. It seems to me
Scarlet not crimson, that anemone :
But there 's amends in the pink saxifrage.
O darling dear ones, let me disengage
You innocents from what your harmlessness
Clasps lovingly! Out thou from their caress,
Serpent! "

         Whereat forth-flashing from her coils
On coils of hair, the *spilla* in its toils
Of yellow wealth, the dagger-plaything kept
To pin its plaits together, life-like leapt
And — woe to all inside the coronal!
Stab followed stab, — cut, slash, she ruined all
The masterpiece. Alack for eyes and mouth
And dimples and endearment — North and South,
East, West, the tatters in a fury flew :
There yawned the circlet. What remained to do?
She flung the weapon, and, with folded arms
And mien defiant of such low alarms
As death and doom beyond death, Bicé stood
Passively statuesque, in quietude
Awaiting judgment.

         And out judgment burst
With frank unloading of love's laughter, first

Freed from its unsuspected source.   Some throe
Must needs unlock love's prison-bars, let flow
The joyance.

        " Then you ever were, still are,
And henceforth shall be — no occulted star
But my resplendent Bicé, sun-revealed,
Full-rondure !   Woman-glory unconcealed,
So front me, find and claim and take your own —
My soul and body yours and yours alone,
As you are mine, mine wholly !   Heart's love, take —
Use your possession — stab or stay at will
Here — hating, saving — woman with the skill
To make man beast or god ! "
               And so it proved :
For, as beseemed new godship, thus he loved,
Past power to change, until his dying-day, —
Good fellow !   And I fain would hope — some say
Indeed for certain — that our painter's toils
At fresco-splashing, finer stroke in oils,
Were not so mediocre after all ;
Perhaps the work appears unduly small
From having loomed too large in old esteem,
Patronized by late Papacy.   I seem
Myself to have cast eyes on certain work

In sundry galleries, no judge needs shirk
From moderately praising. He designed
Correctly, nor in color lagged behind
His age: but both in Florence and in Rome
The elder race so make themselves at home
That scarce we give a glance to ceilingfuls
Of such like as Francesco. Still, one culls
From out the heaped laudations of the time
The pretty incident I put in rhyme.

FLUTE–MUSIC, WITH AN ACCOMPANIMENT.

He. Ah, the bird-like fluting
    Through the ash-tops yonder —
Bullfinch-bubblings, soft sounds suiting
    What sweet thoughts, I wonder?
Fine-pearled notes that surely
    Gather, dewdrop-fashion,
Deep-down in some heart which purely
    Secretes globuled passion —
Passion insuppressive —
    Such is piped, for certain;
Love, no doubt, nay, love excessive
    'T is, your ash-tops curtain.

Would your ash-tops open
    We might spy the player —
Seek and find some sense which no pen
    Yet from singer, sayer,
Ever has extracted:
    Never, to my knowledge,
Yet has pedantry enacted
    That, in Cupid's College,

Just this variation
   Of the old old yearning
Should by plain speech have salvation,
   Yield new men new learning.

" Love ! " but what love, nicely
   New from old disparted,
Would the player teach precisely?
   First of all, he started
In my brain Assurance —
   Trust — entire Contentment —
Passion proved by much endurance;
   Then came — not resentment,
No, but simply Sorrow :
   What was seen had vanished :
Yesterday so blue !   To-morrow
   Blank, all sunshine banished.

Hark !   'T is Hope resurges,
   Struggling through obstruction —
Forces a poor smile which verges
   On Joy's introduction.
Now, perhaps, mere Musing :
   " Holds earth such a wonder?
Fairy-mortal, soul-sense-fusing
   Past thought's power to sunder ! "

What? calm Acquiescence?
　" Daisied turf gives room to
Trefoil, plucked once in her presence —
　Growing by her tomb too!"

She. All's your fancy-spinning!
　　Here's the fact: a neighbor
Never-ending, still beginning,
　　Recreates his labor:
Deep o'er desk he drudges,
　　Adds, divides, subtracts and
Multiplies, until he judges
　　Noonday-hour's exact sand
Shows the hour-glass emptied:
　　Then comes lawful leisure,
Minutes rare from toil exempted,
　　Fit to spend in pleasure.

Out then with — what treatise?
　　*Youth's Complete Instructor
How to play the Flute.　Quid petis?*
　　Follow Youth's conductor
On and on, through *Easy,*
　　Up to *Harder, Hardest
Flute-piece,* till thou, flautist wheezy,
　　Possibly discardest

Tootlings hoarse and husky,
   Mayst expend with courage
Breath — on tunes once bright now dusky —
   Meant to cool thy porridge.

That's an air of Tulou's
   He maltreats persistent,
Till as lief I'd hear some Zulu's
   Bone-piped bag, breath-distent,
Madden native dances.
   I'm the man's familiar:
Unexpectedness enhances
   What your ear's auxiliar
— Fancy — finds suggestive.
   Listen! That's *legato*
Rightly played, his fingers restive
   Touch as if *staccato*.

He. Ah, you trick-betrayer!
   Telling tales, unwise one?
So the secret of the player
   Was — he could surprise one
Well-nigh into trusting
   Here was a musician
Skilled consummately, yet lusting
   Through no vile ambition

After making captive
　All the world, — rewarded
Amply by one stranger's rapture,
　Common praise discarded.

So, without assistance
　Such as music rightly
Needs and claims, — defying distance,
　Overleaping lightly
Obstacles which hinder, —
　He, for my approval,
All the same and all the kinder
　Made mine what might move all
Earth to kneel adoring:
　Took — while he piped Gounod's
Bit of passionate imploring —
　Me for Juliet: who knows?

No! as you explain things,
　All's mere repetition,
Practise-pother: of all vain things
　Why waste pooh or pish on
Toilsome effort — never
　Ending, still beginning —
After what should pay endeavor
　— Right-performance? winning

Weariness from you who,
   Ready to admire some
Owl's fresh hooting — Tu-whit, tu-who —
   Find stale thrush-songs tiresome.

She. Songs, Spring thought perfection,
   Summer criticises:
What in May escaped detection,
   August, past surprises,
Notes, and names each blunder.
   You, the just-initiate,
Praise to heart's content (what wonder?)
   Tootings I hear vitiate
Romeo's serenading —
   I who, times full twenty,
Turned to ice — no ash-tops aiding —
   At his *caldamente.*

So, 't was distance altered
   Sharps to flats? The missing
Bar when syncopation faltered
   (You thought — paused for kissing!)
Ash-tops too felonious
   Intercepted? Rather
Say — they well-nigh made euphonious
   Discord, helped to gather

Phrase, by phrase, turn patches
 Into simulated
Unity which botching matches, —
 Scraps redintegrated.

He. Sweet, are you suggestive
 Of an old suspicion
Which has always found me restive
 To its admonition
When it ventured whisper
 " Fool, the strifes and struggles
Of your trembler — blusher — lisper
 Were so many juggles,
Tricks tried — oh, to soften ! —
 Which once more do duty,
Find again a heart to soften,
 Soul to snare with beauty."

Birth-blush of the briar-rose,
 Mist-bloom of the hedge-sloe,
Some one gains the prize : admire rose
 Would he, when noon's wedge — slow —
Sure, has pushed, expanded
 Rathe pink to raw redness?
Would he covet sloe when sanded
 By road-dust to deadness ?

So — restore their value !
　Ply a water-sprinkle !
Then guess sloe is fingered, shall you ?
　Find in rose a wrinkle ?

Here what played Aquarius ?
　Distance — ash-tops aiding,
Reconciled scraps else contrarious,
　Brightened stuff fast fading.
Distance — call your shyness :
　Was the fair one peevish ?
Coyness softened out of slyness.
　Was she cunning, thievish,
All-but-proved impostor ?
　Bear but one day's exile,
Ugly traits were wholly lost or
　Screened by fancies flexile —

Ash-tops these, you take me ?
　Fancies' interference
Changed . . .
　　　　　　But since I sleep, don't wake me !
　What if all 's appearance ?
Is not outside seeming
　Real as substance inside ?

Both are facts, so leave me dreaming :
   If who loses wins I 'd
Ever lose, — conjecture,
   From one phrase trilled deftly,
All the piece. So, end your lecture,
   Let who lied be left lie !

"IMPERANTE AUGUSTO NATUS EST—"

W HAT it was struck the terror into me?
This, Publius: closer! while we wait our turn
I 'll tell you.   Water 's warm (they ring inside)
At the eighth hour, till when no use to bathe.

Here in the vestibule where now we sit,
One scarce stood yesterday, the throng was such
Of loyal gapers, folk all eye and ear
While Lucius Varius Rufus in their midst
Read out that long-planned late-completed piece,
His Panegyric on the Emperor.

"Nobody like him," little Flaccus laughed,
"At leading forth an Epos with due pomp!
Only, when godlike Cæsar swells the theme,
How should mere mortals hope to praise aright?
Tell me, thou offshoot of Etruscan kings!"
Whereat Mæcenas smiling sighed assent.

I paid my quadrans, left the Thermæ's roar
Of rapture as the poet asked, " What place

Among the godships Jove, for Cæsar's sake,
Would bid its actual occupant vacate
In favor of the new divinity?"
And got the expected answer, "Yield thine own!"—
Jove thus dethroned, I somehow wanted air,
And found myself a-pacing street and street,
Letting the sunset, rosy over Rome,
Clear my head dizzy with the hubbub — say,
As if thought's dance therein had kicked up dust
By trampling on all else : the world lay prone,
As — poet-propped, in brave hexameters —
Their subject triumphed up from man to God.
Caius Octavius Cæsar the August —
Where was escape from his prepotency?
I judge I may have passed — how many piles
Of structure dropt like doles from his free hand
To Rome on every side?   Why, right and left,
For temples you 've the Thundering Jupiter,
Avenging Mars, Apollo Palatine :
How count Piazza, Forum — there 's a third
All but completed.   You 've the Theatre
Named of Marcellus — all his work, such work! --
One thought still ending, dominating all —
With warrant Varius sang, "Be Cæsar God!"
By what a hold arrests he Fortune's wheel,
Obtaining and retaining heaven and earth

Through Fortune, if you like, but favor — no!
For the great deeds flashed by me, fast and thick
As stars which storm the sky on autumn nights —
Those conquests! but peace crowned them, — so, of
    peace!
Count up his titles only — these, in few —
Ten years Triumvir, Consul thirteen times,
Emperor, nay — the glory topping all —
Hailed Father of his Country, last and best
Of titles, by himself accepted so:
And why not?   See but feats achieved in Rome —
Not to say, Italy — he planted there
Some thirty colonies — but Rome itself
All new-built, " marble now, brick once," he boasts:
This Portico, that Circus.   Would you sail?
He has drained Tiber for you: would you walk?
He straightened out the long Flaminian Way.
Poor?   Profit by his score of donatives!
Rich — that is, mirthful?   Half-a-hundred games
Challenge your choice!   There's Rome — for you
    and me
Only?   The centre of the world besides!
For, look the wide world over, where ends Rome?
To sunrise?   There's Euphrates — all between!
To sunset?   Ocean and immensity:
North, stare till Danube stops you: South, see Nile,

The Desert and the earth-upholding Mount.
Well may the poet-people each with each
Vie in his praise, our company of swans,
Virgil and Horace, singers — in their way —
Nearly as good as Varius, though less famed:
Well may they cry, "No mortal, plainly God!"

Thus to myself myself said, while I walked:
Or would have said, could thought attain to speech,
Clean baffled by enormity of bliss
The while I strove to scale its heights and sound
Its depths — this masterdom o'er all the world
Of one who was but born — like you, like me,
Like all the world he owns — of flesh and blood.
But he — how grasp, how gauge his own conceit
Of bliss to me near inconceivable?
Or, since such flight too much makes reel the brain,
Let's sink — and so take refuge, as it were,
From life's excessive altitude — to life's
Breathable wayside shelter at its base!
If looms thus large this Cæsar to myself
— Of senatorial rank and somebody —
How must he strike the vulgar nameless crowd,
Innumerous swarm that's nobody at all?
Why, — for an instance, — much as yon gold shape
Crowned, sceptred, on the temple opposite —

Fulgurant Jupiter — must daze the sense
Of — say, yon outcast begging from its step!
" What, anti-Cæsar, monarch in the mud,
As he is pinnacled above thy pate ?
Ay, beg away! thy lot contrasts full well
With his whose bounty yields thee this support —
Our Holy and Inviolable One,
Cæsar, whose bounty built the fane above!
Dost read my thought?   Thy garb, alack, displays
Sore usage truly in each rent and stain —
Faugh!   Wash though in Suburra!   'Ware the dogs
Who may not so disdain a meal on thee!
What, stretchest forth a palm to catch my alms ?
Aha, why yes: I must appear — who knows? —
I, in my toga, to thy rags and thee —
Quæstor — nay, Ædile, Censor — Pol! perhaps
The very City-Prætor's noble self!
As to me Cæsar, so to thee am I ?
Good: nor in vain shall prove thy quest, poor rogue!
Hither — hold palm out — take this quarter-as! "

And who did take it?   As he raised his head,
(My gesture was a trifle — well abrupt,)
Back fell the broad flap of the peasant's-hat,
The homespun cloak that muffled half his cheek

Dropped somewhat, and I had a glimpse — just one!
One was enough. Whose — whose might be the face?
That unkempt careless hair — brown, yellowish —
Those sparkling eyes beneath their eyebrows' ridge
(Each meets each, and the hawk-nose rules between)
— That was enough, no glimpse was needed more!
And terrifyingly into my mind
Came that quick-hushed report was whispered us,
" They do say, once a year in sordid garb
He plays the mendicant, sits all day long,
Asking and taking alms of who may pass,
And so averting, if submission help,
Fate's envy; the dread chance and change of things
When Fortune — for a word, a look, a naught —
Turns spiteful and — the petted lioness —
Strikes with her sudden paw, and prone falls each
Who patted late her neck superiorly,
Or trifled with those claw-tips velvet-sheathed."
" He 's God! " shouts Lucius Varius Rufus : " Man
And worms'-meat any moment ! " mutters low
Some Power, admonishing the mortal-born.

Ay, do you mind ?   There 's meaning in the fact
That whoso conquers, triumphs, enters Rome,
Climbing the Capitolian, soaring thus

To glory's summit, — Publius, do you mark —
Ever the same attendant who, behind,
Above the Conqueror's head supports the crown
All-too-demonstrative for human wear,
— One hand's employment — all the while reserves
Its fellow, backward flung, to point how, close
Appended from the car, beneath the foot
Of the up-borne exulting Conqueror,
Frown — half-descried — the instruments of shame,
The malefactor's due.   Crown, now — Cross, when ?

Who stands secure ?   Are even Gods so safe ?
Jupiter that just now is dominant —
Are not there ancient dismal tales how once
A predecessor reigned ere Saturn came,
And who can say if Jupiter be last ?
Was it for nothing the gray Sibyl wrote
" Cæsar Augustus regnant, shall be born
In blind Judæa " — one to master him,
Him and the universe ?   An old-wife's tale ?

Bath-drudge !   Here, slave !   No cheating !   Our turn
       next.
No loitering, or be sure you taste the lash !
Two strigils, two oil-drippers, each a sponge !

DEVELOPMENT.

MY Father was a scholar and knew Greek.
When I was five years old, I asked him once
" What do you read about ? "
                                    " The siege of Troy."
" What is a siege, and what is Troy ? "
                                    Whereat
He piled up chairs and tables for a town,
Set me a-top for Priam, called our cat
— Helen, enticed away from home (he said)
By wicked Paris, who couched somewhere close
Under the footstool, being cowardly,
But whom — since she was worth the pains, poor
        puss —
Towzer and Tray, — our dogs, the Atreidai, — sought
By taking Troy to get possession of
— Always when great Achilles ceased to sulk,
(My pony in the stable) — forth would prance
And put to flight Hector — our page-boy's self.
This taught me who was who and what was what :
So far I rightly understood the case

At five years old : a huge delight it proved
And still proves — thanks to that instructor sage
My Father, who knew better than turn straight
Learning's full flare on weak-eyed ignorance,
Or, worse yet, leave weak eyes to grow sand-blind,
Content with darkness and vacuity.

It happened, two or three years afterward,
That — I and playmates playing at Troy's Siege —
My Father came upon our make-believe.
" How would you like to read yourself the tale
Properly told, of which I gave you first
Merely such notion as a boy could bear ?
Pope, now, would give you the precise account
Of what, some day, by dint of scholarship,
You 'll hear — who knows ? — from Homer's very
          mouth.
Learn Greek by all means, read the ' Blind Old Man,
Sweetest of Singers ' — *tuphlos* which means ' blind,'
Hedistos which means ' sweetest.'   Time enough !
Try, anyhow, to master him some day ;
Until when, take what serves for substitute,
Read Pope, by all means ! "
                              So I ran through Pope,
Enjoyed the tale — what history so true ?

Also attacked my Primer, duly drudged,
Grew fitter thus for what was promised next —
The very thing itself, the actual words,
When I could turn — say, Buttmann to account.

Time passed, I ripened somewhat: one fine day,
"Quite ready for the Iliad, nothing less?
There's Heine, where the big books block the shelf:
Don't skip a word, thumb well the Lexicon!"

I thumbed well and skipped nowise till I learned
Who was who, what was what, from Homer's tongue,
And there an end of learning. Had you asked
The all-accomplished scholar, twelve years old,
"Who was it wrote the Iliad?" — what a laugh!
"Why, Homer, all the world knows: of his life
Doubtless some facts exist: it's everywhere:
We have not settled, though, his place of birth:
He begged, for certain, and was blind beside:
Seven cities claimed him — Scio, with best right,
Thinks Byron. What he wrote? Those Hymns we
    have.
Then there's the 'Battle of the Frogs and Mice,'
That's all — unless they dig 'Margites' up
(I'd like that) nothing more remains to know."

Thus did youth spend a comfortable time ;
Until — " What 's this the Germans say is fact
That Wolf found out first ?   It 's unpleasant work
Their chop and change, unsettling one's belief :
All the same, while we live, we learn, that 's sure."
So, I bent brow o'er *Prolegomena.*

And, after Wolf, a dozen of his like
Proved there was never any Troy at all,
Neither Besiegers nor Besieged, — nay, worse, —
No actual Homer, no authentic text,
No warrant for the fiction I, as fact,
Had treasured in my heart and soul so long —
Ay, mark you! and as fact held still, still hold,
Spite of new knowledge, in my heart of hearts
And soul of souls, fact's essence freed and fixed
From accidental fancy's guardian sheath.
Assuredly thenceforward — thank my stars ! —
However it got there, deprive who could —
Wring from the shrine my precious tenantry,
Helen, Ulysses, Hector and his Spouse,
Achilles and his Friend ? — though Wolf — ah, Wolf !
Why must he needs come doubting, spoil a dream ?

But then, " No dream 's worth waking " — Browning
    says :

And here 's the reason why I tell thus much.
I, now mature man, you anticipate,
May blame my Father justifiably
For letting me dream out my nonage thus,
And only by such slow and sure degrees
Permitting me to sift the grain from chaff,
Get truth and falsehood known and named as such.
Why did he ever let me dream at all,
Not bid me taste the story in its strength?
Suppose my childhood was scarce qualified
To rightly understand mythology,
Silence at least was in his power to keep:
I might have — somehow — correspondingly —
Well, who knows by what method, gained my gains,
Been taught, by forthrights not meanderings,
My aim should be to loathe, like Peleus' son,
A lie as Hell's Gate, love my wedded wife,
Like Hector, and so on with all the rest.
Could not I have excogitated this
Without believing such men really were?
That is — he might have put into my hand
The " Ethics " ? In translation, if you please,
Exact, no pretty lying that improves,
To suit the modern taste: no more, no less —
The " Ethics " : 't is a treatise I find hard

To read aright now that my hair is gray,
And I can manage the original.
At five years old — how ill had fared its leaves !
Now, growing double o'er the Stagirite,
At least I soil no page with bread and milk,
Nor crumple, dogs-ear and deface — boys' way.

REPHAN.[1]

How I lived, ere my human life began
In this world of yours, — like you, made man, —
When my home was the Star of my God Rephan?

Come then around me, close about,
World-weary earth-born ones! Darkest doubt
Or deepest despondency keeps you out?

Nowise! Before a word I speak,
Let my circle embrace your worn, your weak,
Brow-furrowed old age, youth's hollow cheek —

Diseased in the body, sick in soul,
Pinched poverty, satiate wealth, — your whole
Array of despairs! Have I read the roll?

All here? Attend, perpend! O Star
Of my God Rephan, what wonders are
In thy brilliance fugitive, faint and far!

[1] Suggested by a very early recollection of a prose story by the noble woman and imaginative writer, Jane Taylor, of Norwich.

Far from me, native to thy realm,
Who shared its perfections which o'erwhelm
Mind to conceive.   Let drift the helm,

Let drive the sail, dare unconfined
Embark for the vastitude, O Mind,
Of an absolute bliss!   Leave earth behind!

Here, by extremes, at a mean you guess:
There, all's at most — not more, not less:
Nowhere deficiency nor excess.

No want — whatever should be, is now:
No growth — that's change, and change comes —
        how
To royalty born with crown on brow?

Nothing begins — so needs to end:
Where fell it short at first?   Extend
Only the same, no change can mend!

I use your language: mine — no word
Of its wealth would help who spoke, who heard,
To a gleam of intelligence.   None preferred,

None felt distaste when better and worse
Were uncontrastable : bless or curse
What — in that uniform universe ?

Can your world's phrase, your sense of things
Forth-figure the Star of my God ?   No springs,
No winters throughout its space.   Time brings

No hope, no fear : as to-day, shall be
To-morrow : advance or retreat need we
At our stand-still through eternity ?

All happy : needs must we so have been,
Since who could be otherwise ?   All serene :
What dark was to banish, what light to screen ?

Earth's rose is a bud that 's checked or grows
As beams may encourage or blasts oppose :
Our lives leapt forth, each a full-orbed rose —

Each rose sole rose in a sphere that spread
Above and below and around — rose-red :
No fellowship, each for itself instead.

One better than I — would prove I lacked
Somewhat: one worse were a jarring fact
Disturbing my faultlessly exact.

How did it come to pass there lurked
Somehow a seed of change that worked
Obscure in my heart till perfection irked? —

Till out of its peace at length grew strife —
Hopes, fears, loves, hates, — obscurely rife, —
My life grown a-tremble to turn your life?

Was it Thou, above all lights that are,
Prime Potency, did Thy hand unbar
The prison-gate of Rephan my Star?

In me did such potency wake a pulse
Could trouble tranquillity that lulls
Not lashes inertion till throes convulse

Soul's quietude into discontent?
As when the completed rose bursts, rent
By ardors till forth from its orb are sent

New petals that mar — unmake the disk —
Spoil rondure: what in it ran brave risk,
Changed apathy's calm to strife, bright, brisk,

Pushed simple to compound, sprang and spread
Till, fresh-formed, faceted, floreted,
The flower that slept woke a star instead?

No mimic of Star Rephan! How long
I stagnated there where weak and strong,
The wise and the foolish, right and wrong,

Are merged alike in a neutral Best,
Can I tell? No more than at whose behest
The passion arose in my passive breast,

And I yearned for no sameness but difference
In thing and thing, that should shock my sense
With a want of worth in them all, and thence

Startle me up, by an Infinite
Discovered above and below me — height
And depth alike to attract my flight,

Repel my descent: by hate taught love.
Oh, gain were indeed to see above
Supremacy ever — to move, remove,

Not reach — aspire yet never attain
To the object aimed at!   Scarce in vain, —
As each stage I left nor touched again.

To suffer, did pangs bring the loved one bliss,
Wring knowledge from ignorance, — just for this —
To add one drop to a love-abyss!

Enough: for you doubt, you hope, O men,
You fear, you agonize, die : what then?
Is an end to your life's work out of ken?

Have you no assurance that, earth at end,
Wrong will prove right?   Who made shall mend
In the higher sphere to which yearnings tend?

Why should I speak?   You divine the test.
When the trouble grew in my pregnant breast
A voice said, "So wouldst thou strive, not rest?

" Burn and not smoulder, win by worth,
  Not rest content with a wealth that 's dearth ?
  Thou art past Rephan, thy place be Earth ! "

REVERIE.

I KNOW there shall dawn a day
 — Is it here on homely earth ?
Is it yonder, worlds away,
  Where the strange and new have birth,
That Power comes full in play ?

Is it here, with grass about,
  Under befriending trees,
When shy buds venture out,
  And the air by mild degrees
Puts winter's death past doubt ?

Is it up amid whirl and roar
  Of the elemental flame
Which star-flecks heaven's dark floor,
  That, new yet still the same,
Full in play comes Power once more ?

Somewhere, below, above,
  Shall a day dawn — this I know —

When Power, which vainly strove
   My weakness to o'erthrow,
Shall triumph.   I breathe, I move,

I truly am, at last !
   For a veil is rent between
Me and the truth which passed
   Fitful, half-guessed, half-seen,
Grasped at — not gained, held fast.

I for my race and me
   Shall apprehend life's law :
In the legend of man shall see
   Writ large what small I saw
In my life's tale : both agree.

As the record from youth to age
   Of my own, the single soul —
So the world's wide book : one page
   Deciphered explains the whole
Of our common heritage.

How but from near to far
   Should knowledge proceed, increase ?
Try the clod ere test the star !

Bring our inside strife to peace
Ere we wage, on the outside, war!

So, my annals thus begin:
    With body, to life awoke
Soul, the immortal twin
    Of body which bore soul's yoke
Since mortal and not akin.

By means of the flesh, grown fit,
    Mind, in surview of things,
Now soared, anon alit
    To treasure its gatherings
From the ranged expanse — to-wit,

Nature, — earth's, heaven's wide show
    Which taught all hope, all fear:
Acquainted with joy and woe,
    I could say, " Thus much is clear,
Doubt annulled thus much: I know.

" All is effect of cause:
    As it would, has willed and done
Power: and my mind's applause
    Goes, passing laws each one,
To Omnipotence, lord of laws."

Head praises, but heart refrains
  From loving's acknowledgment.
Whole losses outweigh half-gains :
  Earth's good is with evil blent :
Good struggles but evil reigns.

Yet since Earth's good proved good —
  Incontrovertibly
Worth loving — I' understood
  How evil — did mind descry
Power's object to end pursued —

Were haply as cloud across
  Good's orb, no orb itself :
Mere mind — were it found at loss
  Did it play the tricksy elf
And from life's gold purge the dross?

Power is known infinite :
  Good struggles to be — at best
Seems — scanned by the human sight,
  Tried by the senses' test —
Good palpably : but with right

Therefore to mind's award
  Of loving, as power claims praise?

Power — which finds naught too hard,
 Fulfilling itself all ways
Unchecked, unchanged: while barred,

Baffled, what good began
 Ends evil on every side.
To Power submissive man
 Breathes, " E'en as Thou art, abide ! "
While to good " Late-found, long-sought,

" Would Power to a plenitude
 But liberate, but enlarge
Good's strait confine, — renewed
 Were ever the heart's discharge
Of loving ! " Else doubts intrude.

For you dominate, stars all !
 For a sense informs you — brute,
Bird, worm, fly, great and small,
 Each with your attribute
Or low or majestical !

Thou earth that embosomest
 Offspring of land and sea —
How thy hills first sank to rest,

How thy vales bred herb and tree
Which dizen thy mother-breast —

Do I ask ? " Be ignorant
    Ever ! " the answer clangs :
Whereas if I plead world's want,
    Soul's sorrows and body's pangs,
Play the human applicant, —

Is a remedy far to seek ?
    I question and find response :
I — all men, strong or weak,
    Conceive and declare at once
For each want its cure. " Power, speak !

" Stop change, avert decay,
    Fix life fast, banish death,
Eclipse from the star bid stay,
    Abridge of no moment's breath
One creature ! Hence, Night, hail, Day ! "

What need to confess again
    No problem this to solve
By impotence ? Power, once plain
    Proved Power, — let on Power devolve
Good's right to co-equal reign !

Past mind's conception — Power !
  Do I seek how star, earth, beast,
Bird, worm, fly, gained their dower
  For life's use, most and least ?
Back from the search I cower.

Do I seek what heals all harm,
  Nay, hinders the harm at first,
Saves earth?   Speak, Power, the charm !
  Keep the life there unamerced
By chance, change, death's alarm !

As promptly as mind conceives,
  Let Power in its turn declare
Some law which wrong retrieves,
  Abolishes everywhere
What thwarts, what irks, what grieves !

Never to be ! and yet
  How easy it seems — to sense
Like man's — if somehow met
  Power with its match — immense
Love, limitless, unbeset

By hindrance on every side !
  Conjectured, nowise known,

Such may be : could man confide
 Such would match — were Love but shown
Stript of the veils that hide —

Power 's self now manifest !
 So reads my record : thine,
O world, how runs it ? Guessed
 Were the purport of that prime line,
Prophetic of all the rest !

" In a beginning God
 Made heaven and earth." Forth flashed
Knowledge : from star to clod
 Man knew things : doubt abashed
Closed its long period.

Knowledge obtained Power praise.
 Had Good been manifest,
Broke out in cloudless blaze,
 Unchequered as unrepressed,
In all things Good at best —

Then praise — all praise, no blame —
 Had hailed the perfection. No !
As Power's display, the same

Be Good's — praise forth shall flow
Unisonous in acclaim!

Even as the world its life,
   So have I lived my own —
Power seen with Love at strife,
   That sure, this dimly shown,
— Good rare and evil rife.

Whereof the effect be — faith
   That, some far day, were found
Ripeness in things now rathe,
   Wrong righted, each chain unbound,
Renewal born out of scathe.

Why faith — but to lift the load,
   To leaven the lump, where lies
Mind prostrate through knowledge owed
   To the loveless Power it tries
To withstand, how vain!   In flowed

Ever resistless fact:
   No more than the passive clay
Disputes the potter's act,
   Could the whelmed mind disobey
Knowledge the cataract.

But, perfect in every part,
  Has the potter's moulded shape,
Leap of man's quickened heart,
  Throe of his thought's escape,
Stings of his soul which dart

Through the barrier of flesh, till keen
  She climbs from the calm and clear,
Through turbidity all between,
  From the known to the unknown here,
Heaven's " Shall be," from Earth's " Has been " ?

Then life is — to wake not sleep,
  Rise and not rest, but press
From earth's level where blindly creep
  Things perfected, more or less,
To the heaven's height, far and steep,

Where, amid what strifes and storms
  May wait the adventurous quest,
Power is Love — transports, transforms
  Who aspired from worst to best,
Sought the soul's world, spurned the worms'.

I have faith such end shall be :
  From the first, Power was — I knew.

Life has made clear to me
   That, strive but for closer view,
Love were as plain to see.

When see ? When there dawns a day,
   If not on the homely earth,
Then yonder, worlds away,
   Where the strange and new have birth,
And Power comes full in play.

EPILOGUE.

At the midnight in the silence of the sleep-time,
  When you set your fancies free,
Will they pass to where — by death, fools think, im-
    prisoned —
Low he lies who once so loved you, whom you loved so,
      — Pity me?

Oh to love so, be so loved, yet so mistaken !
  What had I on earth to do
With the slothful, with the mawkish, the unmanly ?
Like the aimless, helpless, hopeless, did I drivel
      — Being — who?

One who never turned his back but marched breast
    forward,
  Never doubted clouds would break,
Never dreamed, though right were worsted, wrong
    would triumph,
Held we fall to rise, are baffled to fight better,
      Sleep to wake.

No, at noonday in the bustle of man's work-time
  Greet the unseen with a cheer !
Bid him forward, breast and back as either should be,
" Strive and thrive ! " cry " Speed, — fight on, fare ever
      There as here ! "

Printed in the United States
86056LV00006B/278/A